GETTING TO KNOW THE WORLD'S GREATEST ARTISTS

FRANCISCO
GOYA

WRITTEN AND ILLUSTRATED BY MIKE VENEZIA

CONSULTANT SARA MOLLMAN UNDERHILL

CHILDRENS PRESS®

CHICAGO

For four special guys—Mike, Jeffrey, David, and Eric

Cover: The Colossus. 1811. Oil on canvas, 45⅝ x 41⅜ inches.
Prado, Madrid. Bridgeman Art Library/SuperStock

Library of Congress Cataloging-in-Publication Data

Venezia, Mike.
    Francisco Goya / written & illustrated by Mike Venezia.
        p.   cm. — (Getting to know the world's greatest
artists)
    Summary: Examines the life and work of the Spanish
artist, describing and giving examples of his art.
    ISBN 0-516-02292-X
    1.   Goya, Francisco, 1746-1828—Appreciation—
Juvenile literature.   2.   Painting—Appreciation—
Juvenile literature.   [1.   Goya, Francisco, 1746-1828.
2.   Artists.   3.   Painting, Spanish.   4.   Art
appreciation.]   I.   Title.   II.   Series.
ND813.G7V4   1991
759.6—dc20   90-20887
[B]   CIP
[92]   AC

Self-Portrait. 1815. Oil on canvas, 18 x 13¾ inches.
Prado, Madrid. Bridgeman Art Library/SuperStock

Francisco Goya was born in
Fuendetodos, Spain, in 1746. He
was one of Spain's greatest artists
and discovered new ways of painting
that led to the exciting world of
modern art.

The Family of the Duke of Osuna. 1788. Oil on canvas, 88⅝ x 67⅜ inches.
Prado, Madrid. Scala/Art Resource, NY

During his life, Goya painted
portraits of the wealthy people in
Spain's royal court. Dukes, duchesses,
kings, and queens paid Goya to make
paintings of them.

The Colossus. 1811. Oil on canvas, 45¾ x 41⅜ inches.
Prado, Madrid. Bridgeman Art Library/SuperStock

Sometimes Goya made paintings just for himself. He painted things that interested him, and things that came from his mysterious and secret thoughts.

While Francisco Goya was growing up, Spain was a very poor country. The Spanish king was spending most of Spain's money on wars, and the rest went to the king's greedy,

rich friends. Almost everyone else
was very poor.

Cities didn't have garbage pickup
or street lights or police departments.
Roads were rocky and bumpy and
bandits were all over the place!

Regina Martirum. (portion) 1780-81. Cupola fresco.
Basilica del Pilar, Zaragoza. Oronoz, Madrid

When Goya was about 12 years old, his mother and father decided to leave the dusty town of Fuendetodos, and move to the busy city of Saragossa. It was an important move for Francisco Goya.

The city of Saragossa had churches

that were filled with beautiful
paintings and sculptures. Goya
probably saw his first works of great
art there. When Goya grew up, he
painted the walls and ceilings
of some of those churches, like the
one above.

When Goya started school in his
new city, he must have shown a great
interest in art. His teachers thought

he should go to learn about art from Saragossa's master artist, José Luzán.

José Luzán taught Goya to draw by having him copy the artwork and prints of other artists. Goya also made drawings of statues that were in Saragossa. He learned other things that an artist needs to know, like how to mix colors and how to get canvas and walls ready to paint on. After spending four years with José Luzán, Goya traveled to Italy to study the great masterpieces there.

There are stories about Goya's adventures on his trip to Italy. Some of them tell of Goya fighting bulls in different towns along the way, in order to make money. No one knows if these stories are true, but his paintings show that he knew a lot about bullfighting.

The Bullfight. Oil on canvas, 38¾ x 49¾ inches.
© 1980 By The Metropolitan Museum of Art, Wolfe Fund, 1922.
Catharine Lorillard Wolfe Collection

Bullfights were very important to Goya throughout his life. He painted many pictures of them, and made a series of famous prints, too.

During the time Goya was learning about art, a new king started to rule Spain. King Charles III wanted to make things better for his country. He began by fixing up the capital city, Madrid. Soon it was safer to go out at night. Streets were well lighted, garbage was picked up, and new buildings and palaces were built. There were lots of empty walls in the new buildings that needed paintings and decorations. Artists from all over the world came to Madrid to help. Goya got a job there designing tapestries.

Boys Inflating a Balloon. 1778. Oil on canvas, 45¾ x 48⅞ inches.
Prado, Madrid. SuperStock

A tapestry is a beautifully woven cloth that can be hung up like a painting. They were made, during Goya's time, in factories. Workers there copied designs given to them by different artists. The painting above is one of Goya's designs.

Soon people in the royal court noticed Goya's beautiful tapestry designs and asked him to paint their pictures. He was even asked to paint a portrait of King Charles III.

One of Goya's special gifts was his ability to show not only how people looked, but also what kind of people they were in real life.

Charles III. Museo di San Martino, Naples. Scala/Art Resources, NY

Detail of *The Family of Charles IV*. 1800-1801.
Oil on canvas, 110⅜ x 132⅜ inches.
Prado, Madrid. Bridgeman Art Library/SuperStock

Goya liked King Charles III and painted him looking wise and friendly. But he painted the next king of Spain and his queen, above, the way he knew them to be. Even in their fancy costumes, with jewelry and medals, Goya showed them as dull and oafish people.

Francisco Goya loved children. The painting on the next page is one of his most famous portraits. It's fun to look at all the things Goya put in this painting. The hungry cats in the shadows give you a feeling that the boy's pet bird could be in trouble at any moment. Goya found an interesting way to sign his name, too. He put it on the card that the bird is holding in its beak. The boy's bright red suit makes him stand out from the background. But the really special thing Goya did in this portrait was to paint the boy's face so that he almost looks alive.

Don Manuel Osorio Manrique de Zuniga. Oil on canvas, 50 x 40 inches.
© 1983/88 By The Metropolitan Museum of Art, 1949.
The Jules Bache Collection

Francisco Goya was becoming one of Spain's favorite artists.
He made lots of money and had friends in the royal court. Just when things seemed like they couldn't be better, something happened that changed Goya's life, and the way he painted, forever.

Detail of *The Madhouse at Zaragoza*. 1794. Oil on tin, 17⅛ x 12¾ inches.
Meadows Museum, Southern Methodist University, Dallas. Algur H. Meadows Collection

Goya became ill with a mysterious disease, and almost died. He finally got better, but the illness left him totally deaf!

Strange and frightening things began to show up in Goya's work.

He may have painted the things he felt during his illness. People were probably surprised at the new way Goya painted.

Witches' Sabbath 1797-1798. Oil on canvas, 17⅜ x 12⅛ inches.
Lazaro Galdiano Museum, Madrid. Scala/Art Resource, NY

23

Goya didn't put strange and frightening things in all of his work. People still asked him to do portraits and other paintings. Goya's looser, exciting brush strokes gave more movement and expression to his paintings. *The Miracle of St. Anthony* on the next page was done for the ceiling of a church. When you see it close up, it almost looks unfinished, but Goya knew that from a distance his new style would make this painting look more lifelike.

Detail of *The Miracle of St. Anthony*. 1798. 216¾ inches. Cupola fresco.
San Antonio de la Florida, Madrid. Scala/Art Resource, NY

In 1808, Goya's life changed again. Napoleon Bonaparte, a famous French general, wanted to take over Spain. Napoleon sent his soldiers there, and a bloody war began. Goya saw terrible things happening. He decided to show what he saw in his artwork.

Third Of May. c. 1814. Oil on canvas,
105 ½ x 136¾ inches. Prado, Madrid. SuperStock

Detail of the *Third of May* on page 26

The *Third of May* shows Napoleon's soldiers shooting defenseless Spanish people. The fear you can see in their faces and the strong shapes and lighting make this one of Goya's greatest works.

When Goya was older he moved into a large house, and decided to paint the walls there. These paintings were Goya's most mysterious and powerful works. He never told anyone what they meant.

The frightening witches, strange creatures, and people fighting could have had something to do with the way Goya felt about his sickness, his deafness, the war he hated, and his old age.

Above: Detail of *Saturn Devouring One of His Children*. c. 1820-1823. Oil on gesso, 57 ½ x 32⅝ inches. Prado, Madrid. SuperStock

Left: Detail of *Two Old People Eating*. c. 1821-1823. Oil on gesso, 20 ⅞ x 33½ inches. Prado, Madrid. Scala/Art Resource, NY

The Fight With Cudgels. c. 1820-1821. Oil on gesso, 48½ x 104⅞ inches. Prado, Madrid. Giraudon/Art Resource, NY

Francisco Goya lived to be 82 years old. He was able to show the real deep-down feelings of the people he painted in his lifelike portraits.

Detail of child from *The Family of the Duke of Osuna* on page 4

Goya is also famous for the wonderful drawings and prints that he made. Many of them are as hard to figure out as his mysterious paintings.

Tu que no puedes (They can't help it).
Etching and burnished lithograph,
8⅖ x 5 9/10 inches. (plate).
Clarence Buckingham Collection, 1948.
Photograph © 1990, The Art Institute of Chicago.
All Rights Reserved.

Goya painted many different subjects during his life. His beautiful portraits of Spanish life are as interesting as the strange, powerful works he made after his illness.

Detail of *The Meadow at San Isidro.*
1788. Oil on canvas, 17⅜ x 37 inches.
Prado, Madrid. Scala/Art Resource, NY

Modern artists who came after Goya learned much from his exciting and expressive style of painting.

Detail of *Witches' Sabbath.*
c. 1821-23. Prado, Madrid.
Bridgeman Art Library/SuperStock

If you get a chance to see a real Goya painting, expecially the ones he did when he was older, look closely. You can see that Goya did not always paint with brushes. He often used small sticks, or reeds, to slash on paint to get the exciting feeling his paintings are known for.

The paintings in this book are in the museums listed below.

The Art Institute of Chicago
Basilica del Pilar, Zaragoza, Spain
Lazaro Galdiano Museum, Madrid, Spain
Meadows Museum, Southern Methodist University, Dallas, Texas
The Metropolitan Museum of Art, New York
Museo di San Martino, Naples, Italy
Prado, Madrid, Spain
San Antonio de la Florida (church), Madrid, Spain